UARIUM TERRACE BRIGHTON.

Memories and Photographs of Brighton in the 20s & 30s

volume 1

H T Dawes

Contents

Cover : the Aquarium entrance in the 1920s
End paper : Tom Thumb Golf Course, Aquarium Terrace soon after its opening in 1929
Opposite: Scala Cinema, is now Waitrose supermarket in Western Road
Next pages : Greater Brighton celebrations 1928

Brighton Books Publishing

Introduction

Harold Dawes, my father, was employed for most of his life by Walter and Lyn, a wholesale grocer in Jubilee Street. He grew up in Freshfield Street in Brighton, won a scholarship to York Place Grammar School and joined Walter and Lyn in the early 1920s. He worked his way up to be managing director and remained there until the 1960s when the business closed along with all the other wholesale grocers, replaced by the supermarkets. His work in the grocery trade meant that he got to know many shopkeepers and small business people working in the town, and he built up a detailed knowledge of the life of the town between the wars.

His life was typical of the time, working long hours on low wages whilst also enjoying the then limited social life in Brighton - the cinemas and dance-halls. Marriage in the late 1930s was soon followed by a posting to Shimla, an Indian hill station, for the duration of the war. He returned to family life after the war, living in Hollingdean and working in the grocery trade until his retirement. He died in 1992, still living in the same house from which he walked to work in the 30s.

This book has come about, not because of any major event in his life, but because he observed and remembered everything. He had an amazing memory for detail and a fascination for the minutiae of everyday life. His recollections - the two buglers opening Needham's store in Castle Square, the working lives of the carriers based at the Druid's Head public house or the Brotherhood of the Cheerful Sparrows who collected money for charity in Sherry's dance-hall - provide a unique insight into life in Brighton in the 20s and 30s.

He spent many years of his retirement putting his memories onto paper. The material included in this book is mostly based on his own memory backed up by many an afternoon checking dates in the reference library. He was a true Brightonian with a great interest in the town who bought to life a period which was so very different from life today.

This volume concentrates on the areas of the town where the commercial business and entertainment interests were based at a time when many shops and businesses could trace their origins back to the previous century and the expectation was that they would be there for many years to come. Today we no longer have that certainty and it is a common occurrence to find that the shop you thought was there last time has disappeared.

This book brings together my father's recollections of the details and atmosphere of these parts of Brighton with photographs taken at the time. It provides a social history of the town that has now disappeared. A second volume will focus on the back streets of Brighton, where many small businesses were based during this period.

Malcolm Dawes, Brighton 2002

Opposite : Silver Jubilee shoppers in Western Road 1935

Aquarium and the Palace Pier

In the early nineteen twenties the entrance to the Aquarium, with its famous clocks, was known world wide, and could be seen on countless picture post cards sent by Brighton holidaymakers. However, it was losing money and many suggestions to improve its finances appeared in the national and local press.

One proposal to convert it to an underground bus station with gardens and entertainments on top horrified some people, and the consequent publicity helped the attendance figures. During the August Bank Holiday in 1924, over thirteen thousand paid for admission to the Aquarium and Winter Gardens, although it must be noted that it was a very wet week-end causing many visitors to seek shelter.

Eventually it was decided to re-construct the site entirely, and work started in 1927. Two years later the project was completed, at a cost exceeding £100,000, and opened by Prince George. The last part to be demolished was the entrance with the well-known clocks. An American collector acquired a pair of hands from one face; little seems to be known of the fate of the remainder of the building.

Meanwhile the motor traffic grew and grew, year by year. A traffic roundabout, one of the first in the country, was constructed in 1925 between the Aquarium and the Royal Albion Hotel, then owned by Harry Preston. The Southdown bus routes terminating at the Aquarium were moved to Pool Valley in 1929. This came about when the Corporation bought the Royal York Hotel for offices, and leased the basement at the rear to the bus company.

The biggest headache, especially during summer week-ends, was caused by the number of motor coaches bringing trippers by the thousand. As early as 1921, over two hundred coaches were arriving on sunny days. They stopped east of the Palace Pier, the passengers alighted and the vehicles were parked in Madeira Drive near Black Rock until they were brought along in the evening to collect their passengers and depart. The long row of coaches often stretched from Black Rock almost to the Palace Pier during fine days in the summer. They spoilt the appearance of Madeira Drive and obstructed the views of those walking along the promenade.

Horse drawn open cabs could be hired west of the entrance to the Palace Pier for a leisurely and pleasant drive along the length of the town's seafront. Younger visitors could indulge in rides in goat carts available at the same place and bath chairs with attendants could be hired near the Aquarium clocks. The invalid was placed in the chair, blankets were wrapped around, the hood was raised if the weather was inclement, and with the attendant pulling the handle, and devoted relatives assisting from the rear, the procession would move up the slope of Marine Parade. They would pass shoe-shine boys with their footstools advertising Kiwi, Cherry Blossom or Nugget.

Opposite : beach huts, and the Palace Pier, with the West Pier in the distance, in the 1930s. Madeira Drive has been widened near the Palace Pier, the Volks Electric Terminus has been moved away from the road, and the beach huts are about to be demolished to allow further widening of the road and realignment of the railway line.

There was an unusual taxi service available at a rank in Marine Parade near the Aquarium. The vehicles were motor-cycles fitted with large covered sidecar, licensed to carry two passengers side by side.

The Palace Pier was crowded on summer days, when many were attracted by the military bands playing in the Band Stand. The theatre was well patronised and every Christmas staged a pantomime for about four weeks. At the end of the pier on summer evenings, open air dances were cheap and popular.

The iron landing stages at the far end were favourite spots for fishermen, and used by the paddle steamers Devonia or Waverley which came and tied up there almost every day during the summer season. A pleasant afternoon voyage to Ryde and back cost five shillings (25p), and there was time enough at the Isle of Wight to have tea or do some shopping for souvenirs.

Evening trips in the Channel to Beachy Head and back were available almost every evening. A day cross- channel trip to Boulogne, including a short stay at the French port, cost 14/6 (72p).

Below: the Kite Factory Market Street, 15 March 1928. Market Lane was on the right, leading to the Thatched House Inn through which led the old fishermen's right of way. The buildings were demolished in 1939.

Seafront

The beaches between the piers were crowded on fine days every summer, and some visitors went for a short trip on the 'Skylark' owned by Captain Collins, or on one of the smaller craft.

Others tried to find Lobby Lud. When in Brighton his description and approximate whereabouts were given in that day's copy of the Westminster Gazette. Anyone who wished to challenge him was instructed to approach with a current copy of that newspaper and say precisely "You are Lobby Lud and I claim the Westminster Gazette prize".

The prize was fifty pounds and could be larger if no one had won the prize the previous day. As the paper cost one penny, 12,000 copies had to be sold to obtain the prize money alone. He was so popular that special excursion trains were running to resorts when he was due to appear.

Some visitors sat and looked at Roaches kites flying high overhead. Flags were attached to the long holding rope, and advertisements on these could be read as they fluttered in the wind. The box type kites, almost ten feet long and five feet wide, were difficult to handle during changeable weather. One might even fall across King's Road, causing some confusion and the payment of a forty shilling (£2) fine by the Roach family. Their kite shop (opposite) was on the corner of Market Street and Market Lane, south of the Floral Hall and the Wholesale Vegetable Market, opposite the west face of the Town Hall (now Bartholomew Square). By 1930 Mr Roach's business had moved into a shop in Duke Street.

Occasionally a small aeroplane would appear over the beach, and emit a smoke trail spelling out the name of the well-known product being advertised. On calm days the words might remain in the sky for a considerable time.

The children's new boating pool was opened in 1925 on the western side of the West Pier (see page 8), it was so popular that many said it should have been made larger. Later a sunken garden was laid out, almost on the Hove boundary, with pools and fountains.

The West Pier was opened in 1866, and major structural alterations were made in 1890. The pier head was doubled in width, a pavilion was built and a landing stage provided to enable cross channel ships to call. The pavilion was made into a theatre in 1903, and in its early years was occasionally the venue for the earliest public film shows in the town.

The stage plays performed in the theatre in the twenties were well attended, and the West Pier made a record six monthly profit of nearly £15,000 in 1927. Large sums of money were spent on keeping the appearance attractive, and maintaining the structure in excellent condition. Many visitors enjoyed going down to the Fish Market on the beach on early summer mornings, and watching the catch being sold by a method of reducing the prices known as a Dutch auction. In 1923 four hundred persons and over one hundred boats operated from here, the main catch being herring and mackerel. Large quantities were sent by rail to Billingsgate Market in London.

Following pages : the fishmarket in the 1920s

5

The young Prince of Wales, later to be the Duke of Windsor, some times called at the Star and Garter public house, and from a silver pint tankard drank stout laced with champagne, generally know as Bullock's Blood.

Proceeding westward Pallants the costumiers and Duchatel the hosier were passed before arriving at the Old Ship Hotel, which did not occupy the whole frontage between Black Lion Street and Ship Street as there were a few shops at the eastern end.

Findlaters the wine merchants occupied the western corner of Ship Street. Barrance and Ford, specialising in costumes, military uniforms and furs, were west of Middle Street. Between West Street and the Grand Hotel were a large number of small premises, such as shops, clubs, restaurants, a library and the Palladium Cinema. This building had been the Alhambra Music Hall until 1914 when it was converted into a cinema seating two thousand people. It was one of the first to be switched to 'talkies', - films with sound - in 1929.

The western corner of Cannon Place was occupied by Maples furniture shop, and Heppels the chemists adorned by a clock on top. A large post office in Cannon Place was almost adjoining these shops, and nearby in St Margaret's Place stood St Margaret's Church, large enough to hold fifteen hundred worshippers.

There were many streets between Western Road and the seafront which disappeared with the building of Churchill Square and its car parks. Grenville Place was the continuation of Cranbourne Street after crossing Upper Russell Street, and contained some attractive late eighteenth century houses on the lower side (see pages 10 and 11). Those on the opposite side had mostly been converted into delivery entrances for the Western Road shops.

Upper Russell Street sloped down from the eastern end of Western Road, and turned westward where it joined Russell Street, ending near Russell Square. From this road Artillery Street and Cannon Street were turnings on the southern side.

Kidd and Hotblack operated the large Cannon Brewery between these streets at their lower ends. This firm supplied many public houses which, being painted red and black, were easily recognisable. The business was acquired by Tamplin & Sons in 1927.

In the mid-nineteenth century there were ammunition stores in Artillery Street, and in the basement of the Grand Hotel where they could still be seen in the 1930s. They were connected with the West Battery which stood on the seafront until its removal in 1858.

The Sussex Cold Store was in Russell Street and in the vicinity were many firms of meat importers. A large number of smaller streets in this district, between West Street and Cannon Place, such as Bodle's Court, Blucher Place (see page 12) and Wellington Place, have also disappeared. Among the many public houses hereabouts were the Boatmen's Arms, the Fisherman at Home, the Flowing Tide and the Fire Brigade Arms.

Opposite : the boating lake by the West Pier opened in 1925

GRENVILLE PLAC

Western Road

At the eastern end of Western Road between Upper Russell Street and Clarence Street, there were over twenty shops, which were demolished when Churchill Square was built. Starting with Dudkins the furriers, others were Kendall's the umbrella makers, and Salmon & Gluckstein the tobacconists.

Beyond Clarence Street, Dawkins the drapers had a long frontage facing a narrow section of Western Road. The road was so narrow that two oncoming motor buses had difficulty passing; with their wheels almost on the narrow pavements, shoppers were swamped on wet days whenever buses passed. Conditions improved when four business premises on the northern side of Western Road were acquired by Johnson's the furnishers, and rebuilt further back.

Lee & Sons the constumiers and the large millinery and drapery stores of Hetheringtons were beyond the Castle Street turning, together with Chipperfield & Butlers, dealing in drapery and soft furnishings.

'Vogue, Value and Variety' was the selling slogan of Plummer Roddis Ltd, milliners and ladies outfitters, who had an extensive frontage from Western Terrace almost to Montpelier Road. The acquisition of the Premier Fur Stores during the late twenties enabled the firm to complete their ownership of the whole block of buildings.

Returning eastward on the northern side of Western Road, the large Employment Exchange occupied the eastern corner of Montpelier Road. This location must have caused inconvenience and a good deal of walking for the many unemployed people in eastern Brighton.

The nearby Scala Cinema was opened in 1907 as the Electric Bioscope (see photograph opposite the title page). Bon Marche had extensive premises near the corner of Spring Street. Boots the chemists traded in old premises between Spring Street and Dean Street, but these were demolished and the entire block re-built in 1928.

In the next section the eastern corner with Crown Street belonged to Stafford's (see page 15), probably Brighton's first department store. Re-building of this block was the first step in the Western Road Widening Improvement Scheme which was later to alter entirely this side of the thoroughfare. Stafford's new premises were opened in late 1926.

East of the Marlborough Street turning, Johnson's the furnishers extended their premises, and completed the re-building in 1929 in time to celebrate 25 years of trading in Western Road.

Meanwhile Woolworth's had also expanded by taking over an adjoining wallpaper firm's premises. All articles in Woolworth's sold for three pence (1p) or sixpence (3p), although more could be paid for items such as fireside companion sets by buying each component separately. Brigden's motor car salerooms stood on the western corner of Regent Hill with Wade's premises on the opposite corner.

Previous pages : Grenville Place, now Churchill Square, demolished 1965 and 1967

Opposite : Blucher Place 1930s, now Churchill Square, demolished 1957

13

Marks & Spencer's store was situated next to Woolworth's but moved eastwards next to the Imperial Arcade around 1931.

In the upper section of North Street, which then ended at Upper North Street, Smithers had offices on the southern side with their brewery at the rear, but in 1923 part of the premises were demolished, and the imperial Arcade built through to Western Road.

Further up North Street - now Dyke Road - on the upper corner of the junction with Regent Row, Mr. Hazelgrove operated a blacksmith's business known as Ye Old Forge which dated back to 1745. The Hazelgrove family took over in 1810, but transferred the business to Centurion Road in 1932. Old Mr. Hazelgrove died in the following year aged 86, and was buried dressed in a Sussex smock with white socks, and old custom in his family.

Between the Imperial Arcade and the eastern end of Western Road, there were twelve business premises including Athelatan Woods who specialised in men's wear. There was also a public house called Malster's Arms. At the far end, the main window of Fowler's grocery shop faced straight down North Street. A large advertisement for Bovril stood on the roof.

Above : Staffords, Western Road 1930, with the new Boots premises behind

Opposite : Boots, Western Road, Christmas sale 1926. The new Boots store was built on this site east of Spring Street

Following pages : Jubilee celebrations in Western Road in 1935. The rebuilding of the north side is nearing completion with the new Marks and Spencer behind the last old shops in this narrow section

15

WESTERN RD BRIGHTON 1935 (2)

Brighton Railway Station

Brighton Station always presented a busy scene as summer approached - on Easter Monday 1927 over five hundred trains arrived, and during the August Bank Holiday of the same year three quarters of a million passengers passed in and out. Thirty-two crowded special trains from London arrived on August Monday in 1924, when a total of nearly ninety arrived over five days. It was by far the busiest seaside station in the south as shown by some statistics released by the Southern Railway, which had in the early 1925 grouping superseded the old London, Brighton and South Coast Railway. During a ten week seaside season in 1925, seven million passengers were carried to many resorts between Margate and Bournemouth, and of these, two million came to Brighton.

A new train was started in late 1925 to satisfy the needs of commuters going to London Bridge Station. There were individual lights over every first-class seat, and for those wishing to work, tables were available to be stowed away when not required. Facilities for washing were provided in every coach, with a supply of hot and cold water.

The railways attracted the public with excursion trains and cheap day return tickets. On certain days of the week, a day return from Brighton to London cost 6/4. (32p), and for those who preferred shorter journeys, a day return to Lewes was one shilling (5p), Hassocks eleven pence (4p), Steyning one shilling and four pence (7p), and Tunbridge Wells four shillings (20p).

Travellers approaching the station from Trafalgar Street had been able to enter the station by going through a doorway immediately above the goods yard entrance gate, and climbing fifty-nine steps. They then had to cross the dangerous main access road inside the station it they wished to reach the booking offices and main line platforms.

This stone stairway was closed in the late twenties, and a passage way with only twenty-four steps giving direct access to the concourse was opened. Other changes were the construction of improved toilets, brighter refreshment rooms, and better booking offices. The stone platform at which trains on lines three and four now arrive and depart had an inset track between these lines in the twenties. This single track recess was used by trains to the Devils Dyke, the buffers some distance down the platform from the ticket barrier being hidden by a bookstall which was rarely open.

In the thirties, electrification and twelve coach trains to London necessitated longer platforms and this caused a tapering effect which squeezed out the inset track. The journey to Devil's Dyke was very popular in the summer at a fare of eight pence return (3p), and hundreds of people were to be seen every hour leaving the train at the Dyke station high up on the downs, and wending their way up the winding rough road to the top of the hill.

To cope with the increasing traffic in buses and motor taxi-cabs using Queen's Road to the station, the approach to the southern end of Surrey Street was rounded and widened in 1921. At the northern end, the Terminus Hotel was demolished in 1924 to ease the bus problem, and Junction Road was made to join Queen's Road with Terminus Road.

Opposite: trams at Brighton Station 1930s

QUEENS ROAD. BRIGHTON.

Queen's Road and West Street

On sunny summer days Queen's Road was thronged with day visitors who had just alighted from the numerous excursion trains. There were over a dozen public houses between Brighton Railway Station and the bottom of West Street, so while the mothers and children soon reached the beach, many husbands stopped for liquid refreshment, and assured their wives that they would soon rejoin them. Some did not emerge until half past two, when the public houses closed.

The silent movies, as they were then called, had greatly improved technically since the early short comedies, and the new longer films had become extremely popular. To meet the increased demand, large picture palaces were being erected in the bigger towns. The Regent Cinema was built near the corner of Queen's Road and North Street, and opened on the 26 July 1921. Costing £400,000, it was described as a Wonderland among Kinemas, with its coloured marbles, its fantastic lanterns and its gleaming lights which had brought a welcome touch of brightness to this drab highway. Armchair seats were available from one shilling (5p) upwards.

Some of the best known screen stars became household names; these included Bebe Daniels, Pola Negri, Clara Bow, Tom Mix and Jackie Coogan, while for those who liked comedy Buster Keaton and Harold Lloyd were popular.

There was also the Regent Restaurant, where luncheons at 3/6 (17p), and dinners at 5/6 (27p) could be digested while listening to Louis Lewis's Orchestra. For those unable to pay these prices, the Ship Cafe provided lighter meals up to 11pm.

Later the Regent Dance Hall was built over the cinema, and opened on 10 December 1923. it was the largest dance hall in the world to be constructed above ground level, and fifteen hundred dancers could enjoy themselves without overcrowding. 1s/6d (7p) and 2s/6d (12p) were the usual charges, but on Fridays when evening dress was essential, the admission price was raised to 3/6 (17p).

The Regent Cinema suffered a severe fire in early 1929, and was closed for about six months, during which time it was converted to show films with sound tracks (known as talkies). On 1 July 1929 the Regent Cinema was re-opened with the presentation of the talking and singing epic 'The Singing Fool', starring Al Jolson. Before the end of that year, two more Brighton cinemas were showing 'talkies' and the silent screen days were numbered.

On the eastern side of Queen's Road, above the North Road turning, stood the Sussex Eye Hospital, founded in 1832 and containing 30 beds. On the same side of the road between North Road and Church Street turnings stood the Oddfellows Hall. Built in 1833, it was large enough to seat 250 persons, and was often hired for concerts, balls and lectures.

Most of the visitors making for the beach walked down the west side of West Street, passing the many eating places and public houses, the best known being William Harris's

Previous pages : Queen's Road in the 1920s

Sausage Restaurant, the King's Head Hotel and the George Hotel. The last named was almost on the seafront, standing on the corner of a little turning called Kent Street.

The King's Head Hotel was near St Paul's Church, and was a very old hostelry said to have been the last resting place of King Charles II before he fled the country from Shoreham following the execution of his father.

West of West Street there were numerous narrow dingy streets and alleyways, many running through to Russell Street, but the district was purchased by Brighton Corporation in 1929. Soon after the gradual widening of West Street began with the demolition of many properties and the consequent disappearance of many street names such as West Street Cottages, Chuter's Gardens and Bunker's Hill.

On the eastern side of West Street above the Duke Street turning was the Eight Bells Public House, while just below the turning was Christies Hotel owned by Edlins, an Irish family with a number of licensed premises in the town, all situated in busy thoroughfares and with competitive prices, their houses were well patronised.

Nearby was the office of the Brotherhood of Cheerful Sparrows which collected large sums of money for charity either with fancy dress dances at Sherrys, two day gymkhanas in Preston Park, or flag days. The local branch had more members than any other in the country. Above the Boyces Street turning the Academy Cinema was the largest picture palace in the town before the opening of the Regent Cinema. On the east side, near the south end of West Street stood a building well over one hundred years old. The double bow fronted house was entered by climbing a flight of stone steps was used as offices by the Brighton and Hove General Gas Company.

The next building as one approached the seafront was Sherrys Dance Hall, a popular meeting place for young people. The many dancers on the floor could be viewed from the balcony while enjoying a tasty cup of coffee for a total outlay of sixpence (2p).

A Saturday dance there in September 1925 ended soon after midnight, and smoke was seen two hours later. It seemed the fire started in the kitchen under the balcony, and the main damage was caused by smoke. The local paper stated that the ornate panelled walls of cream and apricot, embellished with gilded cupids, floral scrolls and oval mirrors, were blackened, and the firemen's hoses flooded the billiard saloon in the basement.

Following pages : West Street with the George Hotel on the left

626. WEST ST. BRIGHTON.

AVERY'S. B'TON.

North Street

In the early twenties Hanningtons premises on the southern side of North Street did not include those on the corner of East Street, but they did have an undertaking business on the opposite side adjoining Lloyds Bank.

The latter was vacated when the northern side of the street was rebuilt to allow the roadway to be widened., this enabled Lloyds Bank to enlarge their premises. Hanningtons extended to the corner of East Street when premises occupied by Treachers Library and Glaisyer & Kemp the chemists were taken over. Hanningtons attracted a high class clientele, and at sale time rang their best customers to give details of the most popular reduced items. All their linen was made in Lancashire or Ireland.

The Countess of Huntingdon's church, built in 1871, was on the south side of North Street facing New Road. Between this church and Meeting House Lane stood one of Lesson & Vokins shops, the other being on the corner of Ship Street. During the twenties they became Vokins when Mr W T Lesson became the proprietor of a large store at the top of North Street known as Sopers.

The Clarence Hotel, built in 1785, was well patronised by commercial travellers, who stayed there when calling on tradesmen in the town and district. Teetgens were further up the street, and there the aroma of freshly roasted coffee from the shop pervaded the atmosphere, and those who liked a leisurely cup in pleasant surroundings visited he adjoining cafe. Joseph Lyons, who already had a restaurant near Hanningtons, opened another above the Ship Street turning which provided waitress service - these young ladies in their distinctive dress were known as 'nippies'. The lower corner of North Street was occupied by Joseph Smith Ltd, drapers and silk mercers, and adjoining was the Princes Cinema, once called the Bijou.

J Baker & Co, tailors and outfitters, were on the upper corner, but this side of West Street down to Cranbourne Street was set back to widen the roadway in the late twenties. A branch of Montague Burton's the tailors was built, another branch had already been opened next to the North Street entrance of the Regent Cinema.

The large Sopers emporium was situated further up North Street, almost in Western Road. It specialised in drapery, silks and ladies garments, and every year had a grand Yuletide display of toys with the most elaborate Father Christmas department in the town.

On the north side of North Street below the King Street turning stood the imposing red brick buildings of the Prudential Assurance. They were set back from the adjoining premises making the narrow highway a little wider for a short distance.

A little further down the street a narrow passage way led to the Athenaeum Hall, which could seat almost five hundred people, contained an organ and was the home of the Brighton School of Music. The Spiritualist Church held trance addresses and clairvoyance frequently, and for those with more earthly tastes, there was also a billiard

Opposite : North Street, 1928

salon. Adjoining the Midland bank, situated on the upper corner of Bond Street was the De Lux Cinema opened in 1908.

The building on the lower corner of North Street and Bond Street had been occupied by a firm of auctioneers for over two hundred years, and a cottage at the rear was even older, but in 1922 the site was cleared for the National Provincial bank to be erected. The Salem Baptist Chapel in Bond Street, dating back to 1776, adjoined the new bank premises.

The stretch of pavement in front of the few shops situated between the bank and Clarks the bakers on the corner of New Road was covered by the Royal Colonnade, but that attractive feature dating back to 1823 was demolished during one week-end in late June 1929.

North Street below New Road was narrow, particularly so below the Chapel Royal where Galliers shop premises were set forward so that the western wall faced up North Street. The firm sold electrical items and wireless sets. During the 1929 Parliamentary elections, an enormous board affixed to the wall showed the latest positions of the parties while loudspeakers announced the latest results as they became available. large crowds gathered on the pavement and spilled over onto part of the road. Arrangements were made to continue the service throughout the night, while Sherrys in West Street gave results between dances to an accompaniment of cheers and boos.

A journalist working at the Brighton & Hove Herald offices in Princes Place near the Chapel Royal, in the early twenties, was distracted by continuous music, most of it discordant. In North Street there were barrel-organ grinders, one stringed fiddlers and unaccompanied vocalists singing out of tune, while pupils practised on the Chapel Royal organ.

Other unemployed men played various instruments in Western Road, where prosperous local tradesmen complained that the noise kept customers away. Some of those who had been heroes when in the trenches realised that they had become unwelcome beggars. There was even a Council proposal in 1921 to abate the noise by means of a bye-law, but the Home Office vetoed it.

Opposite : The Electric Shop, looking east in North Street in the early 1920s.

East Street to Middle Street

The shops in East Street catered for those with more expensive tastes, who were able to park their cars easily in a thoroughfare free of buses. There were no parking restrictions and most motorists stopped outside the shop they wished to visit.

Dutton & Thoroughgood's on the corner of Castle Square and East Street was one of five of their shops in which fine footware was sold, including locally hand-made boots measured to the customer's requirements.

On the same side of East Street, near the southern end, stood the premises of Hudson Brothers, stocking a wide range of grocery lines, many unobtainable elsewhere. Personal service was most important; assistants carried out the purchases which were placed carefully in the limousines by the chauffeur.

Cutlers the hairdressers were nearby, and members of that family had three salons in the street. Business boomed as the new shorter hairstyles for ladies became fashionable. The bob was popular in 1922, followed by the shingle two years later. In the late twenties the even shorter Eton crop was favoured by the more daring young ladies, and when some began to wear trousers, critics grumbled that it was difficult to tell the men from the women.

Brill's Baths datng back to 1869 were near the seafront, but they were demolished in 1929 when the Savoy Cinema was built on the site. It was the first large cinema to challenge the Regent, and specialised in midnight matinees one night of almost every week.

Lyon & Halls shop on the western corner with the seafront, sold pianos, gramophones and a wide range of records. Among the popular tunes of the day were 'My Blue Heaven', 'Me and My Shadow', 'If You Know Suzie', 'I'm Just Wild About Harry', 'Ma, He's making Eyes At Me' and 'What'll I Do'.

On the western side of East Street, Warden's Buildings was the first turning north of Bartholomews. About forty yards long and wide enough for a large lorry to negotiate, it ended at the loading bay entrance of Wallis, Holder & Lee, the wholesale grocers with offices in Market Street, near the rear of the Sussex Hotel. The premises were demolished at a much later date, and together with Warden's Buildings became the Regent Arcade.

The Druid's Head public house in Brighton Place was used as a base by many carriers covering a large part of central Sussex. Messages were received there, either by note or by telephone call, and each carrier was informed where to pick up parcels before setting out for the day. Each covered a district - Payne went to Albourne and Bolney, Oostick to Hurstpierpoint and Burgess Hill, Shergold to Haywards Heath, Warden to Partridge Green and Cowfold, Coleman to Steyning, Isted to Lewes, Chailey and Barcombe; while Koppett went to Rottingdean.

Opposite : Pavilion Buildings in Castle Square in 1928, 8-11 Westminster Bank, 12 Jons gowns, 13 Susses Goldsmiths, 14 Norwich Union Fire Office.

The Hippodrome, Bulwer Avenue

They often also used their vans for other purposes, such as collecting milk from farms and moving furniture, so some limited their journeys into Brighton to three a week. A parcel weighing 56lbs would usually be carried for about ninepence (4p).

The Central Police Station was situated in the basement of the Town Hall with the entrance facing east. Those in custody or on remand were escorted upstairs to the Magistrates Courts in the same building.

Even those charged with minor misdemeanors who who were fined ten shillings (50p) or less, were told when sentenced "or seven days in custody". They were then promptly ordered to the cells, and stayed there until someone paid the fine or the sentence was completed. Short sentences up to about one year were always "with hard labour".

Everyone tried to keep out of trouble. News of a court appearance spread quickly, and as soon as it reached the ears of an employer, dismissal was almost certain, even when the offence was not connected with the firm. It was difficult enough for honest folk to obtain employment; the position of those with criminal records was hopeless.

Queen Mary often visited the Lanes, taking a particular interest in the antique shops. Sometimes she bought an object or etching connected with the Royal Pavilion, and occasionally would donate one of her purchases to the town.

As private telephones were a rarity, relatives sent urgent messages from other towns by telegram. Many were distributed every day all over the Brighton area, and these were carried from the General Post Office in Ship Street by uniformed telegraph boys on red bicycles. Each one wore a belt with a buttoned pouch in which the telegram was carried. On warm days the boys sat on forms on the pavement on the southern side of the building, where the recess in the pavement is considerably wider. Every few minutes a man came out of the Post Office side door with a telegram, gave it to the next boy and ordered him to deliver it as soon as possible.

The Hippodrome in Middle Street opened in 1901. In 1906 a seventeen year old beginner named Charlie Chaplin appeared there with Fred Karno's company. He stayed in 'theatrical digs' in Tidy Street.

Top of the bill stars in the twenties included Marie Lloyd, Nellie Wallace, the young Gracie Fields, Will Fyffe, Sandy Powell and Ernie Lottings. The normally large audiences appreciated the double acts of Scott and Whaley, and the singers Layton and Johnstone, while Tubby Teddy Brown playing his xylophone, and Jack Payne his new BBC dance band were firm favourites with many patrons. There were two performances every week day at 6.15pm and 8.45 pm, with matinees Wednesdays and Saturdays.

Opposite: the Hippodrome in Middle Street

Old Steine and the Royal Pavilion

In the early twenties wireless sets with frequent time and news programmes were owned by few people, so hardly anyone knew the precise time. Everyone relied on Lawsons clock in Old Steine which was always right and easily seen by all (see page 32).

Lawsons the jewellers stood on the southern corner of St James's Street, and the upper section of the western window facing across to Castle Square was filled with the face of a clock which measured about three feet in diameter. For those unable to see the clock, a large bracket hung from the corner of the premises, and from it was suspended a giant pocket watch complete with a gold chain.

Needham's (see page 39) was a large store on the northern corner of Old Steine and Castle Square, and announced its opening every day at nine o'clock when two buglers on the roof sounded the 'Salute'. Passers-by then knew that they would be welcomed in to see the wide range of clothing which included plus-four suits considered ideal for sports wear.

When the Old Steine Gardens were thought to be the most suitable place to erect the War Memorial to commemorate the Brightonians who died in the Great War of 1914 to 1918, the large statue of King George IV - the Prince Regent - was moved from there to a new site at the south end of Church Street near the North Gate of the Royal Pavilion.

Below: Armistice Remembrance Day 14 November 1936

The statue was placed in an upright position on a trailer, and slowly towed the short distance, which fortunately was level.

On Armistice Days, as they were then called, traffic in Old Steine was gradually reduced and then stopped. Tillings buses were not allowed to cross into Castle Square and all trams were turned at the loop at the southern end of the Victoria Gardens.

A huge crowd gathered at Brighton's new War Memorial, which in 1922 was unveiled by Lord Beatty. In 1924 the number present was estimated at fifteen thousand stretching from Edward Street to Sam Isaacs Restaurant on the corner of Marine Parade.

The service was always held at the eleventh hour of the eleventh day of the eleventh month, and as the two minutes silence started, the silence was intense, as throughout the town everyone and everything stopped. Many who stood there bareheaded in the autumn sunshine had vivid memories of Flanders and the Somme.

Many Indian Army units suffered severe losses on the Western Front in France and Belgium during the Great War of 1914 to 1918, and large numbers of wounded were brought to Brighton for medical treatment. The Royal Pavilion, the Dome and the Corn Exchange became a military hospital, while on the lawns between were erected many large huts for convalescents and administrative purposes. During a visit by King George V and Queen Mary, numerous medals were presented including one Victoria Cross. The ceremony was watched by one thousand Indian wounded, attendants and nurses.

Many patients died from wounds. Hindus were cremated at a ghat on the open Downs north of Patcham, the services being conducted with strict observance of the religious beliefs of the dead. A marble chatttri was erected on the spot after the War, and unveiled by the Prince of Wales (later the Duke of Windsor) in early 1921. Muslims who died were taken to a cemetery at Woking.

The entire Pavilion grounds and buildings of the temporary military hospital were enclosed by high boarding attached to the railings to prevent any unauthorised person getting in. The whole effect must have bees extremely drab and unsightly. After almost six years the War Department opened the gates in June 1920 so that the public could walk through the inside road. The Dome was also handed back and by November was again available for functions.

In late October 1921 the Maharaja of Patiala unveiled the South Memorial Gate of the Pavilion dedicated to Brighton in memory of the Indian soldiers who were nursed there in the Great War. I remember standing in a line of schoolboys on the southern side, but cannot recollect anything that happened on that day, or how we all got there.

The old gate dating back to 1633 had been removed. Many said that they did not regret its departure as it resembled a sentry box, but old photographs give it a pleasing look, showing ornamental gates flanked by open ended buildings crowned by ornate domes. Between 1921 and 1923 many improvements were made, the railings and shrubberies were cleared away, and on the eastern side the present ornamental balustrade was built.

On the nearby corner of Marlborough Place stood the entrance to the Blenheim Hotel. Over the years the hotel had extended into adjoining houses in Church Street; these fine residences were built on part of the site of the infantry barracks demolished in 1670. Troops stationed there probably supplied guards, sentries and escorts when the Pavilion was a royal residence during the reigns of King George IV and his brother King William IV.

Crabbs Wine Store on the western corner of Church Street and New Road stocked the widest range of imported wines in the town. Large casks were delivered to the cellars, where wine was bottled, corked and labelled, before being stored in dark alcoves until required in the shop.

A number of strange implements are probably still there, including a metal candle holder with a handle about two feet long. This was used when locating bottles; electric light bulbs gave too bright a light, and were said to have a harmful effect on the wine.

The cellars extended under the pavements of Church Street and New Road, where a passage led eastward towards the Dome. This was believed to be a secret passage used when wine stocks at the Royal Pavilion needed to be replenished. I have seen the entrance to the passage in the wine cellar, but it was blocked by empty cartons. There may have been a permanent barrier behind them.

The Prince Regent certainly had an interest in the property as his signature is on a conveyancing document dated 1808. In 1929 when Queen Mary made a private visit to the Royal Pavilion, she walked through to the Dome along an underground passage dating back to 1777.

Roller skating could be enjoyed at the Corn Exchange in the late twenties, for an entrance fee of one shilling per session, including the use of skates. The hardwood floor was considered to be the best in the country, and the men glided around attired in plus-fours or evening dress to the music from a gramophone amplifier.

Almost opposite in Church Street stood the imposing showrooms of the Brighton & Hove General Gas Company, which were brilliantly illuminated by four huge gas-lit bowls of light, two suspended in front of each window flanking the main entrance. There were 32 mantles in each lamp. In 1928 the Gas Company had 65,000 customers between Lancing and Telscombe. This building housed the Local Studies Library until 2002 and is due to become a public house as part of the Jubilee Street redevelopment scheme.

The road at the side of the building led to the large Gas Company yard which is now occupied by the Prince Regent Swimming Pool. The large red brick building east of the Gas Company premises was the Brighton County Court for civil actions. It was used in recent years as storage for the library opposite and will soon become offices for the museum.

Barbers Restaurant, in which moderately priced meals were served on two floors, was on the western corner of Church Street and Jubilee Street. The front of the adjoining building, built in 1829, resembled a church and was occupied by the Central School, and Pells the printers.

The school with its large pointed Gothic doorway and dark interior could not have given a reassuring feeling to the young children entering it. The playground was almost completely roofed by buildings above, and had a high wall with grilles on the side facing Jubilee Street. Sunshine and fresh air reaching that play area must have been minimal.

On the opposite corner of Jubilee Street, the Palace Yard adjoined the rear of the Waggon and Horses public house. Jubilee Street was very narrow for a short distance near that point, and was nicknamed the bottleneck. Inside the Palace Yard, which was enclosed by a stone wall and large wooden door, there were a number of small business premises including the milk depot of Wyatt & Sons. Milk bottles were loaded in metal crates, not in plastic containers as nowadays, and damaged crates were mended in a welding workshop on the premises.

During the twenties many gifted actors and actresses appeared on the stage of the Theatre Royal, including Lilian Draithwaite, Phyllis Neilson-Terry, Seymour ???Hicks, Cedric ???Kardwicke and Tom Walls.

Between the Theatre Royal and the Unitarian church in New Road was the Court Theatre, the first in Brighton to go over exclusively from stage shows to films in 1906. Capable of seating an audience of fifteen hundred, it suffered a major fire in 1923 and was demolished in the sixties to make way for offices.

Above : closing down sale Needhams department store on the corner of Castle Square and the Old Steine 1930

The Victoria Gardens

The Victoria Gardens date back to the Queen's Diamond Jubilee in 1897, when they were opened to the public after being laid out and planted. Enclosed with high railings, with numerous seats along the paths in each park, they became a quiet oasis in the centre of the town. Changes came in the early nineteen twenties when Captain Maclaren(?) became superintendent of Parks and Gardens. The encircling railings were removed and the new outside path was loose shingle. After a great deal of criticism, coloured paving slabs were laid in late 1928.

Grand Parade, Marlborough Place and Gloucester Place were all two way roads The tram, kept to the extreme left, so that passengers boarded and alighted on the garden side of the road. When one way traffic was introduced in 1926, that arrangement persisted for a while resulting in trams alone facing all oncoming traffic. It was obvious that this could not continue for long, and in May 1929 the trams were reversed so they were on the right of traffic, that solved one problem and created another. It was too dangerous for the passengers to alight in the road, so the driver opened. the door behind him, so they used the front platform instead.

Early morning trams up to about eight o'clock turned at the Pavilion loop, not going on to the Aquarium. The tramways had a special arrangement for passengers to and from Brighton Railway Station. A ticket to the Aquarium, bought on any route, allowed the holder to alight at North Road, and board a station tram. That conductor had a punch which cut a 'T' for through' in the ticket and no further payment was necessary.

The gardens were brightly illuminated in 1928 for the greater Brighton celebrations. Strings of electric light bulbs were hung from tree to tree, while the exterior of some trains were ablaze with coloured lights. These illuminations started at the Palace Pier and followed the valley right through to the eastern side of the Level ending near Elm Grove.

The grounds surrounding St. Peter's Church were enclosed with high railings, and the public were not allowed to enter them before 1899. In 1922 the railings and shrubberies were removed.

It was said that the Level was owned by no one, so everybody ignored it. It was a sea of mud every winter with just a few blades of grass surviving. On Guy Fawkes night bonfires were lit everywhere; ashes and partly burnt pieces of wood lay about for months. The central walk from Southover Street to Oxford Street had a tarred surface with no flower beds. That walk looked even worse when the Open Market operated there for a few years in the early nineteen twenties. In the spring the rooks started building nests in the tall elm trees. There were dozens but they have all disappeared owing to expanding Brighton being built over their old feeding grounds.

The fencing encircling the Level was removed in 1923, and an outer path laid out a few yards from the roads. During 1929 the southern section was made into a children's playground with a boating lake and stone bridges at a cost of £5,000. It was opened a few days before Christmas in the same year.

Memories and Photographs of Brighton in the 20s & 30s by H T Dawes (2002)
ISBN 1-901454-05-3 @ £6.99 + £1.50p p & p.
First published in 2002 by Brighton Books (Publishing)
c/o ETP, 9 South Road, Brighton BN1 6SB
Phone & Fax: 01273-542660. email streetwise@pobox.com
Printed by Delta Press, 2 Goldstone Street, Hove BN3 3RJ

Acknowledgements: photographs lent by : Chris Horlock and Jacqueline Pollard, with assistance from Robert Jeeves of 'Step Back in Time', 25 Queens Road, Brighton.

Design by Selma Montford

Brighton Books (Publishing) have published the following books:

no 1: 'The Vanishing Villas of Preston & Withdean' by Selma Montford, Jacqueline Pollard and Robert Sanderson (1996) ISBN 1-901454-00-2 @ £5.50

no 2: 'Dr Brighton's Indian Patients' by Joyce Collins (1997) ISBN 1-901454-01-0 @ £5.50

no 3: Photographic Memories of Brighton & Hove by Mark Whenman (1998)

ISBN 1-901454-02-9 @ £2.50

no 4: Little to Spare & Nothing to Waste: a Brighton Boyhood in the Hungry Thirties by Robert Hayward (1998) ISBN 1-901454-032-7 @ £5.50

no 5: Hilly Laine to Hanover: a Brighton Neighbourhood by Lavender Jones and Jacqueline Pollard (1999) ISBN 1-901454-04-5

Available, by post only from the address above, or from good bookshops

The following book is also available from Brighton Books (Publishing):

'Blighty Brighton' (1991) about Brighton in the First World War ISBN 0-904733-55-6

@ £4.95

Please add £1.50 per book, £2 for 2 books or more, for postage & packing. Cheques should be made payable to Brighton Books (Publishing) with the cheque card number on the back.

Below : ticket to Sherrys Dance Hall. End paper : Western Road and Imperial Arcade 1937

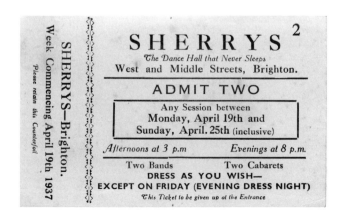